AF268759

ENDLESSNESS IS NO DESOLATION

Elisabeth Workman

"The real apocalypse comes, not with the vision of a city or kingdom, which would still be external, but with the identification of the city & kingdom with one's own body." *The apocalypse lays bare the mystery of kingship; stripping off the Emperor's New Clothes, to reveal the harlot. Kingship is fornication—the identity of politics & sex. In the apocalypse the walls do fall; the walls separating inside & outside; public & private; body physical & metaphysical.* –Norman O Brown, *Love's Body*

Lucile is suddenly there with her 'Long live the king!' // After all those words on the platform (the guillotine, mind you). –Paul Celan, "The Meridian"

BAN THE NUDE WITCH SHOW

I cut. I cut & I have to go back.
In offering to the public these volumes
of vexed objectivity I cut. Don't you mean
subjectivity? That's history's hex. Don't
you mean sex? Don't take it personal

scaffold-romance-captivity wants
a very clean cut with reticules
for catching animalcules but I feel
a flashwound in dirty repetition
hackjob drama of splay & seepage
a fail mass I emerge a hot messy more
of a sobject from the gauche spot
with corrupt happy clouds & jellyfish &
the other night deer
when they were sleeping
I dreamt I held you in my harm

u r my   my only

when   when

how much

how much   how much

u r my   my only

what's the use
of a hole
if it's just
an end?

in a silent one I find
a ticket stub for passage
from voluptuous panic
to prenatal fantasy walden and back
wards facing words
facing vast

tea beside the sea
of ferns   sun ra
& desert eros   why not
repopulate loneliness
(there are so many of us)
its ceremonial swelling
with sounds to spell
a slogan it's a spell
sound it out

LABOR FOR LABOR THE MARKET'S FIXED

         alphaboding
          a fugitive anxiety

      American people   as if they're
missing or hiding & she's calling as in come hither: *Peeeeeeeeeee—pole!*
         in a nascent language
The American people sounds like
cock
continuously

         & fork collapses *fuck*wards

a is for abracadabra
b is for box
Hey, mama cocks!
Do you have a fucked-tongue, too?

it crows for warp from the halfmast of a soundtrack already wrecked when cut reveals
  a peep-hole

  & them went down into the deeps

Good morning, rank perfume.
Here's an aggressive hope for corrupture
                              while the world hyperventilating.
evicts tender rot, its humid breath

laps at our edges, its hempire   a silence regarding us.   a ring around
our rose-fingered sleep

ANY ORDINARY, LONG-WINDED DELIRIUM WILL DO

a great demand   & a rule that anyone
          for order   draped over the

                                                      gate is gathered

    this effort coupled with

          wild &   u   after contact after rapacious power   reaped
    a fine crop   shadow red shame
                      hear-say trees   a clear cut
divides   T &/or F: The first symptom of American equality was soldier.
                                                      parable
production. Fields & fields of fucking up. Even sleep can't escape them, so why not

                                                taint
                              (like rot)

          the brands that seal
our edges the portion of them
surrounding us like recidivist bureaucrats   powering around our red
          delirium. Specimen of the whole. Not national
ACCIDENTAL in the headlights, the suicidal fauns, the wide periphery

MISTY CRASH DERBY

They sprung & vaulted
over each other's   cul-de-sacs   fur cliffs where energy gets stuck
or
if shaken goes ballistic. This is my   great hip

these Kentuckians are full of light.
a number of combustible   infinite hips   spun from blood
each womb bomb tore our attention to   oblivion.

That's almost it.

f a k e   i t ?

When our bodies crash there's a sound of

tinkling.   god
twirls a small white handkerchief

something   convulses
in the wind   a carnal knowledge sound effect
clamoring to ride shot-gun
through the angsty forest. God is something that goes off. It basically says birds slash
through the canopy like pulsing assassin
bitches then nods in silence from deep fur lining.
There are bones in the corsets & bones of the   burned
on the beach & tiny feet & dainty hands
splashing in cookie sales when no one was there to say watch who you work for

cage by cage
caves within caves
the tail inside my

DOGS   they get stuck &

at one point today I queefed on god

& he gave up

the ghost & all of my languorous witch whiffs floated in the azure air

what goes on between us

Bang me   What goes on between us   seen

growing in water   golden guns on a fuck plate

                                         bingbingbingbingbingbingbing chora red

Roman candles burning bipolarly a rolling country.   *HERDS &*

FLOCKS THE FLYING SAUCERS   longing

camps in their voracious   swallowing   god of

parasites   god of plastics

                        god of naughty picnics
      Ohio would be perfect   I was told to pin up ripped-out hearts to

the sky right down to the last minute. In my own chamber   you can

make anything up whenever light or air are wished for

                        "Come in."   "Are any of you ill?" he began.   yes &

these mawberries taste us as we chew them

                                                                  how

many play dead   drinking the tone of things   drunk in dread   while glimmer holes

                                         bloom children pure terror

& your eternal forest the plot in which

The plates stacked   among the rocks are for hurling at the witness trees, they

dream propulsion. It's a game. . . a dead endlessness.   The more you

do it the more your body will go on without you

There's no blue distance to the whole machine.
We're now set to frolic until

all of us its

shadows

Body bags by the bye & bye. All animal wants are supplied

GO A LITTLE AWAY

HISTORY OF A DAY'S TANTRUMS.   first
SWIVEL CHAIRS ARE
ABOUT ASSHOLES! ASSHOLES ARE ABOUT THE ROTTEN SUNS INSIDE ME!
ROTTEN SUNS ARE ABOUT BLACK HOLES! BLACK HOLES ARE ABOUT THE
PATRIARCHAL FEAR OF PUSSY SODOMY DEATH DIFFERENCE & MUTATION &
MUTATION IS ABOUT THE MAGIC OF DEATH! KNOCK THREE TIMES FOR DADDY
ISSUES. KNOCK FOUR TIMES FOR MATRILINEAL MASOCHIST SELF-SACRIFICE.
MY MOMMY I ADORE / MY BABY I AMORE! KNOCK INCESSANTLY FOR LOVE'S
TRAUMA IN THE EMERGENCY ROOM OF TIME.

For some reason
I couldn't communicate that before without dripping, but now I'm totally okay
with duration
except in taverns & bored rooms, where I'm fighting with a despot over the size of the
soul & I know the despot is really me & I am really not-me in some kind of postponed
allegory   engorged
green colloidal intensity
to tarry there was not to feel at home through which we travel is
to all we have left. Engine cocktail total
silence superficial
glacier special
needs legitimate
institutions
rape comparison
not withstanding
what's the use
of a ramrod
a laborer
a mother

The greatest difficulty in organizing a family establishment is   moonwalking without
skin [abrasions, for example, blisters brushburns amputations decapitations etc.]
                    a whole class of young women getting help

HUNDREDS OF HALF-NAKED GIRLS
IN A TIME OF BADNESS taint Friday night in a yellow
dress pleated with red roses. I will be

     a limbless doll whore & you can be a monster truck & this can be the mucus plug
that pops out when I am run over   We can call it chapter 6
     the teaching quote hospital all

   natural disposition training for feral tots

         & so we cleft.
         Friday night is alright
It may be called bad taste   a dirty horde   but this is yours

free-for-all night ~~pudding~~ secretion party

Is it still hymen to you in your country where strangers are felling your woods?

   The point being
this cold storage is   business
It grows membrane & still & the evening quiet alone watches over our cells

     We might   more than anything need
where public ventilation has to stop, there
tumescent conspirators   the loud battle cry of dead
girls rubbing
against hot phones
     how to hold
        how to call the smash cuts
        how to fork for hours unadorned
        thought tongue cunning
     The greatest difficulty for the greatest generation is fang
adaptation   remote-sex-cum-ground-control-cum-drone-driver hazing & rackets
the women basically herd together basic military training it
is obvious   errata: chapter 6:

It always appeared to me that they remained together as long as they could bear it then
they rose   en masse
     ALARMS GO OFF WHEN THEY EXIT THE BUILDING

I take a brick from childhood .

You must be bored out of your pants

        not quite fat

                              Heat lifts its heavy skirt

                                the lima-bean

                        the far off sea

                        almost total flower

                        keeping

                                a let-down cow

SWOLLEN MORNING OVERSLEPT HIGHWAY
spellmasters go under
snort the circuitry
rewired just started to write required
here for you to redacted

the skirt lifts its boredom to show you
this ectoplasmic nun fetus coming
out of rehab which makes
listening
to philosophers so great
a treat. I smite
the great doom
for doldrums. Americans
love talking
kingking
ing
ing

.

. . . . . ing guh. ing ing gah. ing ing ish. *NOT WITHOUT A FEELING, PUN PUNS* in

inglish pls! sing dingding fwiw, king of meh, pls excuse my inglish. . meh king um ing . .

you make you himming you hawthing you pigeoning you hamming you pig eons you you

didn't read the father poems he saiding did you you didn't read the shit about new snow

for the rich you didn't $UBMIT you didn't delicate touch in the seminal pool the gated

communithing jacking & offing off inging & &ing & you'll never be able to host right &

now

you have to ringtone from that impoverishment dingding & you have to norm a cling

...object pokes object... licks its static bingbingbing can you look it I bet you like it kingky

at the locks of your enclosure till you

socket watch & ticking till you gut the feeling right on the wasted beach who *didn't*

read the father poems enduring many epochs without wearying ing who made lush folly

in the dim sublimity spilled death juice in the gazing go go beeee dahhhh go be dah

yolo yum go be da mamama I don't know anymort mort mortal toy ill go car pay die um

I don't know anymore if-ing e-wing keep rewarding the same thing the same ing-thing

I love some melancholy wand dingding I'm wearing one right now

dingdingding but keep yr purell yr pure hell

to yrself all you masters touching the unknown like golfers fucking crab holes in the sand

something in the hollow aiding the view in a pinch:

hey lala hey nonny nonny hey yala hey go-be-dah yala lalala

what they would never see period

after period gone

missing & miss

THE WATER CLOSET [A white-tiled restroom in the Inglish Factory. There are stalls, & toilets in the stalls, but in an effort for greater transparency, the doors have been removed.]

Miss Invisible [as a continuous voice whispering over an intercom]: . . . plus flesh saw plus starry placenta plus ovular burst plus sea rat secretions plus interposing spindles of dew plus ...

Pussy Wallow [walking in, looking up, around, at the voice]: Mom?

Tyrannica Wrecks [close behind]: Don't be such a pussy. Mom's dead.

Miss Invisible: . . . plus pus moth plus orb plus melancholy jelly plus dross plus lowercase o plus blade plus bladder plus waterfalls the falls. . .

[sound of toilet flushing]

Inglish Head [speaking from stall in the far corner]: Your mother was a typical case, a narcissistic bird of paradise, a hot mess in a basketcase.

Pussy Wallow: I think you mean BIRD OF PARADOX. & who are you?

Miss Invisible: . . . plus mucus plus bile a while plus spastic majestic biodomes plus blood oath plus . . .

Inglish Head: I'm the risk averter, the deviance-converter, the proto-prick, the reprimander, the symptom-tracker, the empirical anthologist, the ing decider. I am, in a word, the last word on any matter.

[sound of toilet flushing]

Miss Invisible: . . . plus sad cells plus lace crawl plus lasso plus laceration plus vein plus clot plus scab plus . . .

Tyrannica Wrecks [seeing head emerge from stall]: But you are just a floating head with a flaccid tail! ... Are you a tampon or butt plug?

Inglish Head: Good Taste consists in the appropriate manifestation of faculties in their proper season & degree; & this can only take place when they are so inculcated that there is no tendency for any one of them unduly to rebel. They serve the head—the only true master—agreeably.

Pussy Wallow: Please hurt me now; my ing is rigor morting.

Inglish Head: A prime symptom of an out-of-balance faculty is the diminished capacity for amusement.

I NEVER SAW ANY PEOPLE WHO APPEARED TO LIVE SO MUCH WITHOUT AMUSEMENT

they were told there
would be no math here one hour late the headmens who can't count right they were told
you are the best the headmens who can't cunt who say true & cantos
they were told true or false the blue book comes   from blue trees

that is a retro
the main cunt con   druid plumage

they were told to just point & moot you can't talk everythings
they were told to ply in the pillage to sit & wait & hate each other fidget conduit &
wait & count trees minus trees always equals fixed ings of monuments

they were told there would be jetpacks

to apex in I

not come back

not say dead   lay dead

they were told speak this that we may give you time & we will shew you houses
& they were told just paint the houses

& they were told nice patio

& they were told nix excess

fix the grids & syntax deviations   (devilmations)   ((cloven nation))
& they
were told no image that fur feels brains miasma-land or returns hot pincered cinder
speech with flesh noise & skull quivering under thirsting was okay

they were told latex sentence
prick the pathos
to   quaint   hummmmmmmmmmmmmmmmmmmmmmmmmmmmm
mmmmmmmmmmmmmmmmmmmmmmmmmmmmmmmmmmmmmmmmmmmmmmmmmmm
they were told but nobody was listening nobody was listening nobody was listening nobody

nobody was radiant

nobody was here

THEY WERE TOLD POSTERITY but time

       in spite of its invisibility is
       so sensitive it
       implodes

       in nap stuff
       a see-through
       paparazzi

       fight or flash
       hind or flight

       in the middle
       of summer
       wide open
       a colossal hole
       spits split
       tales to swallow

       sum futu

       re:

defined again a hymn was sung come! come! come! while it continued the "anxious
beaches" flapping their highways going ahead without them the polyamorous magma
somewhere far below bleeding tension poles their thrumming a full throttle wobble
the perceptible young children trying on dead animals at rest stops when they say you're
not doing it right not like that no no you have to hole the soft parts a hole is to see to be
the mass of some great mamminal & when one tripped & fell into another what's a body
to me but a pause I never go to see where it ends as if everyone is really waiting for the
next century already dead it fills a few hollows & makes beds for the swallows solomon
always cries his father said & there seems to be some confusion as to which century
this is dear morning creatures faces full with scenes

plus cyst urn plus sanguine parlor plus glistentubes plus rubyrash plus zeitgeist
ooze plus spoon oz plus loose fuzz plus glisterine plus selective fatigue plus scare
rush plus scar pits plus wombcrucible plus sunsteeple plus ash plus plush mush
plus sky lance plus vanishment

BIRD OF PARADOX sez   you may follow me by the S's I make

process is a   moodiness

straddling irrational lexical momentum
chapter 9 house I wake up in a very bad modern   the idea of it
all dependency returned to an island they had left & now felt indefinitely alone

I SHOULD HAVE LIKED EARLY

MORNING CATHARTICS

                        process is a   moodiness
                                                  in
                                    the idea of it

                              thoughts on the subject of female
education   the dismal
twinkle judging by this criterion   cloister—rampion—locks & locks
        to be seen at a dis-tressing rate   loin taken with claw & sugar   makes
excellent crow moms
bring terror home; if it rains, sloth mom, if it blows,
        a mass of overgrown invasive moms   implode the atrium
from within   it seems hardly hair to marionette scarcity hardly fair to my
cavalier studies in self-immolation but I am sure   *I SHOULD HAVE LIKED EARLY
MORNING CATHARTICS*

I SHOULD HAVE LIKED EARLY MORNING CATHARTICS

"Wanted, immediately, 4,000 fat hogs."

wilderness
in the
the idea of it

self-immolation   *I SHOULD HAVE LIKED EARLY*

MORNING CATHARTICS

whisperings in the dumpster

all lattices of hesitation to be pulled down by
invasive crawling networks of the underneath   always roiling or just always there,

at any point an emoticon encircles suburban overstraining.   sarcasm the intercom
unqualified praise of country   if every sentence did not end with "I am clean,"
electric tentacles supplied the debt

momentum bitches

&

waves

the tension

swaying houses

a psychic state of
want

as in I want to rite the pig

straddling irrational lexical momentum

                                            now felt indefinite

    write the
    ready
                   the terrible

polydynamic   tensions

                        loin

          a psychic state of gazing upon   distance
       with emollients. Wanted, immediately,

the heard rot grotto of the poem
        networks of the underneath   always
there,

                            "I am not clean,"

         a quivering hormonal pig
                 Shakespeare is obscene
          mistress & minstrel   in the shape of
stolen bread. I once went into the cottage of a country

& wet the bed while
reading a book of desolation
throbbing   in crowds   I must make
                        a replica pleasure.

I once

went into the cottage of a country

& wet the

d   e   a   d

first it is warm then it gets

cold blaze of dream skin whose words when they are urgent or delight or accidents or
recurrents how first a step sets trespass on fire brushing against a snout fresh dripping
then it gets colossal this interdiction forever mounting an age we had to cross, at its foot,
houses moving from place to place, the big one, blind pig blind pig, slit the skin to pour
me out some mass echo of pussy pressed into the pink bank back, "help," I'm flowery,
I'm inelegant, I'm too much flowing backwards, lowing fucked words, stepping into
jawbones, a still warm stream snaking out

out out a reason for this blood-letting like you are clawing fate while complicating
universal ruths.   observations on roles state them here   ergo trolls
ergo enlightenment attached   to its own brand of self-
medication opposite itself   a sealed arena or a
cialis or a discipline or even a catoptric house cat I haven't yet decided this is a delicate
ruth   whoever harms one will have terrible things happen to him. A hand or
leg or foot becomes completely dislocated & leaps from a cliff. Chasm data, it is said.
On one edge farce & the other protest & the betweens its wide open gush
        keep going you are not missing anything
this morning I myself could barely make sense of my body
                                                        one leg at a rhyme. these
                                        paragraphed on limbs. skin spouts on the
                                        stun the site of sacred confusion (her
                                        house)

a mitotic totem of fresh wounds
                        oozes
                        warm feelings

                                                prim trollops keep twitching
inside me I should never have discovered this vast empire waist
        in the roiling cuntry
        I AM ALWAYS ALREADY LOST

                        crux & luster alchemical must

almost every master you meet will tell you rev rev rev & purrr your hobble bot their
boasted independence proof poof in boots proof positive habit hobby horse (her house)—
shhhhhhhh the laws are half-asleep

almost every master you meet will tell you dream hard war plots to hardware some kind
of hardwire mary, marry, christen, & carry, bury among abundant overgrowns
                                        gorge us & confective puke whooshing half
awake gowns sucked through the turbine festoon the treeline—what happened to ruth? I
think she is my fanny

a clusterfuck in the mist
                                                        ohmama give
no fancy parties without ecstatic caterwaul & pay no priests elsewhere (her house)
                                        one way to do this everyday is
to relearn people upon earth
        to hear clamor

to her clamor

close cutting till *THE WHOLE BLADE SEEMED AMICABLE*

It is certainly possible quim gong bell jar upon a hill are you coming tumbling
down I feel a dropsy grammar gathering in the head these unreliable sources
incontinental mapping

locus suspectus "the warm room & the unhymen afternoon"

fugue state I wanna free dissolute habits state slit here again assent to the
does not assent to the infidel but ill atone for want of sate & warship

calamity then an old newspaper
haunted dainty
daemonic namby pamby

The common course & byproduct must be both belonging & non-longing; it can take a
couple of weeks before she's able to hobble again. In the hands of every tinker & tailor
self-stimulation alone is like a brave banner, embroidered with a device of her own
imaginings. In order to break her of the habit, pulp it.

In a slightly different sense: "I feel unhymen, well, free form fear."

As to exactly what my thighs were thinking contracting fanciful variations, any
transatlantic circulation might inspire morbid imaginations in Europe as well as America,
so as to come across a concealed world.

"The place was so peaceful, so lonely, so shadily-un-hymen."

aristocarcasses low & illiterate in such a world must ever return here, the dead domain
pooling redacted fits to turn such feelings into a holesome enervation in a fresh cut baby
way.

"The in- & outflowing waves of the current, dreamy & lullaby-unhymen."

It wrote of wet immensity.

I wrote immediately:

AS A SPECIMEN OF THE DURATION in which the knowledge pulpit is ground with everyday intolerance & fear of ████, I will transcribe the notes I took of a conversation, at which I was present.

Dr. Hat: I wish that you would explain, Ms. P, what you mean by ████. I know it means something of persons, things, sense perceptions, but that is all I know.

Bird of Paradox: Eyes ex, Dr. Hat, vats plume, widows tisk, laugh at me. I'm hysterical.

Dr. Hat: Well, but what is ████?

Bird of Paradox: It is difficult, very difficult to close these mauve glow heights; to sacrifice blowsy underscores whose poles are confounded. A ████ queen thrusts elephantine hatchlings not tourniquets; a burnt abattoir haunts the horde's people in the land of taint, & it mediates silence.

Dr. Hat: But what is it the people mean by talking of feeling the ████? & waiting in ████ for the ████? & the extacy of the ████?

Bird of Paradox: Oh Doctor! I am afraid you are a pellet! A tufa gnome of astral undertow, etc. This is gore insurance, a slash-ay of the never clear coven, the beating of the lamb-view, the welcome of the sop cloven, it is the essence of ugly love, it is the flounce of glo-wrist beings in jellyfish; it is the jelly-being in us, it is talking the hole ghosts into our cleavage, insisting hours slip down basin gods, it is a blurry cow, it is eating & drinking & sleeping in the cloud jelly, it is bleary lines in the fat night, it is bending low & mere & catastrophic, melancholic in the smite state, smitten in the cut place, it is bonking mctcors in thc puffs of scum without proof, without—

Dr. Hat: Thank you, Ms. P. I feel a weird pellet of ████ that is turning on me & terrifying me. I think we could clean this up & really flip it into something big, like a cruiseship or a cruise missile or a waterpark or parking lot!

Bird of Paradox: How overeaten you are! how penitent shark co-zee!

Dr. Hat: But I thought this was about ████.

Bird of Paradox: Or is it now about blind idolatry supplanting missionaries cantering with the converted as the whole world bank overheats & recharges teenagers in the notching year?

Dr. Hat: I've already done so with several women, including myself, & we don't abuse the liberty. Otherwise, what is there—endlessness?

plus the fetus was delight plus pimp plus poet plus puffer plus trust plus surge
plus player plus saucerorbs plus orgy whisps plus guiltbeggarskirt plus amo squirt
plus squeegee thee plus squandered thine plus scarlet patch plus briarsnatch plus
uppercase A upside down like a bullshead like a cosmic uterus plus

In the distance a party of don'ts humps the ridge
                                We can make out
theatrical contracts   capes chariots dynastic tentacles coquettish pleats & pleats   lit
from a certain angle

                                         (in a blind-spot
                                       a cataract)

                                        a cataract
they try to contain with the dictum we can agree to dis
            pose   we can agree to dis
            associate here's a doe-nation   pick pert daisies from eyepits in the
        wasteland   stare down a hole
shot throo & drift out public speaking balloons?
                                    a blue sold over lasts to haunt

          gore lore spun   between us   heaves in span
                              of collapsible bridges
                                                 billowing highways into bedrooms
               there spreading apart the iridescent sheets of a nascent morning
          a superlunar flowerbed wet with breath needs
nerve goo to get a cow across
          to grow a crow across to come

with a misconstrued message of pieces from the other side
which might explain *DO YOU HAVE PERMISSION FROM THE OWNER OF THE ALLEY TO BE HERE?*
which might explain the whole onward crush
which might explain the orange smoke seeping from vents
as an appropriation of the invisible regions of infernal girls
which might explain middle management offing each other in the wings &
antlers & heels thrown higher than the head & shoulder pads
I puddle
I pore to sweat in the wetlands of Walt Whitman skullfucking thrones
—who can deny his capaciousness?—
while in the pit the conductor frantically searches for his cue
which might explain I repaired to the forest to shoot naked children & wild animals

how they didn't respond
how I was embarrassed how
to answer how
I was embraced by counterfeit in the frothy night

I know where is a hind

         &I depart myself repeated in that reaching
I lack you   is the first contact
        foaming in the round
an airy carcass party in a mouthfelt open
     cuz I love the rash & I lack
        like a sun crisis   it looks like it has melte[d]
& mad[e] a hole   where people go to eat roses & hold ices

    a perimeter
under the leaves
            the sounds

                akimbo
   a feeling   member   violet   in
   amusement. iridescence a kind   muse
     a sensitive
        system

       for
ETHEREAL INDUCEMENTS
    like heavy-lidded

       dew.

           the constant
pleasure
    an infant
     instruction—
        uttercups, the subject being   into pleasing

[pause]

the curtains open to reveal

            the head   shiny

     in search of some essential music
       a citizen depends upon
          to
eat

edges without

                 flickering
   everyone should have a song that should please   a cloud

               to a   seashore

going away & returning   they grow up in moats just
under the leaves
          after the sounds

                              akimbo
feeling across   violet edges
          a kind of curtain a muse meant
          but we're so landlocked
     a parody of

     form
ETHEREAL INDUCEMENTS   step over the
     heavy-lidded dromedaries

                                        the author aimed
at depicting

     pain   to hear the constant   hiss of god taste
               —as if to justify
                                        annihilation
                                        discipline your
     subject   the bitter object suckling   etcetera

[pause]

the curtains open to reveal
                    (disguise   )
& the problem of

               incessant
                    applause   bones
&   membranes

          a citizen   cloak
                                        about
          the threat of contingence
     outside
          its edges
     the great American star.
               you can tell she is fingering her
throat
          in a loud way   in the mirror

a perimeter for going away & returning where they grow up in moats just
under the leaves
looking after the sounds
surround "I do not want to forget"
limbs akimbo
to get a feeling across   to re-member   violent edges in the absence of every
other amusement. iridescence a kind of curtain a muse meant   breakfast
was a sensitive beach but we're so landlocked   the
███ system's a parody of itself
more phantom members
form
ETHEREAL INDUCEMENTS   you have to step over the dead bodies all the time
like heavy-lidded dromedaries in the prophylactic aisle
lounging in the leatherette decompression chamber
downing mountain dew   the author aimed
at depicting authority

it was painful to hear the constant anesthetizing hiss of god taste—it was
a pleasure   —as if to justify
an infantilized entirety   much cheaper than annihilation there's some kind
of instruction—   discipline your syntax, little fucked-
up buttercups, the subject being the bitter object suckling doomlets into pleasing etcetera

[pause]

the curtains open to reveal fanny
flanked by piglets   (disguised as ███)
& the problem of sacrifice

"for they would
not bear it"
the splitting was incessant
higher than the head   applause   expressed by knocking shinybones &
humping thin membranes
in aisles in search of some essential music
but fanny says a citizen depends upon the noise the citizen makes. cloak me
in slayer shirts & enroll me into the bore lodge to think about
the threat of contingence how
to an outside dissolving
its edges without control-alt-delete   [pause]
the third act opens to reveal fanny
indecipherable feeling you can tell she is fingering her hem flickering in &
no it is her throat everyone should have a song that should please her yes in a
cloud way in the gutter realm in a loud way in the tatter reel in a breath is the
ghost way in the mirror war the no world—ALARMS
some apology to a conceptual seashore

ETHEREAL INDUCEMENTS

ALARMS we were margins we were
monstrous / the infinite was breathing us

*I CONFESS I WAS
SOMETIMES TEMPTED TO
SUSPECT THAT THIS
ULTRA REFINEMENT
WAS NOT VERY DEEP
SEATED.
IT OFTEN APPEARED
TO ME LIKE THE
CONSCIOUSNESS OF
GROTESQUERIES TRYING ON
VEILS*

for the preservation of flowers
the mothers squat
out of the picture

DANGER OF RURAL EXCURSIONS

FOR THE PRESERVATION OF FLOWERS, MOMMIES SQUAT & SHARD

THE MOMMIES SCRAWL, THEY SLIME CRAMPED SPACE, THE SURFACE
GLITTERSICK WITH THEIR MUCUS

FOR THE PRESERVATION OF FLOWERS, THE MOMMIES IN THE
GUTTERS SCATTERED THEIR STRANGE CONSTELLATIONS IN PLEATS &
PILE

CONVULSING A SILENT PAST, THEY PISSED THE PAST LINE & SAW
THEMSELVES IN TWO

IF YOU ARE ALWAYS GAZING UPWARDS
YOU MISS THE BLOODY SHOW

FOR THE PRESERVATION OF FLOWERS
ANYONE WILLING TO EAT DIRT MOTHERS

ANYONE WILLING
TO HEAR DEATH
IN THE DEPTHS OF THEIR
ETERNAL FORESTS
THEIR SOIL LUNG
THEIR HOT MASS
THEIR DECAY
MOTHERS

stellar corpse *YOU*

tortureplex of pulsing gargoyle nutrition *ALWAYS*

these soft luxury anguish machines *LIVE*
     a bloodbath in the drawing-room, a coffin of fixity coming

down *AGAIN*

ENDLESSNESS IS NO DESOLATION, as our little village was called
                    a violet sensorium of the disordered
                                        pendulum
                                        strung from knocked up ruins
here ornate heads hackle like spiked ghost blossoms to rupture a lifelong static quote
leafy life forms fall from above as we push through air   crowned
& compelled by an unknown momentum   as long as you keep moving
you can't stop

ENDLESSNESS IS NO DESOLATION

                    if I err in this distance it is merely evidence of
a capricious submission to survive

                           this moment circumscribed by my
own delusion of its fixity. Oh where is my gypsy knife tonight? paternalisms reassertions
malingerers joy-free impregnation. I raise my feet against it ill I say, excuse me, but
before you insert that space probe, I'm going to read you a poem. I'm going to meet you,
ever bred & buttered (not to mention bodied) to say mother broke
my mother bore back racked & broke the terminal mechanism. Attention mechanics, if
good workmen, uncertain of employment, bend into the widening loam
                  above the sunken city of a dead (domi)nation

ENDLESSNESS IS NO DESOLATION

            Giant pupils from the future will cite penal, industrial repression!
         a site sutured the more important parts of wife & mother with muzzle &
muffler to cut(up)lass
confusion   oh where oh where
                except by eye-witness
          This is my wide-legged stance watch whole caravans pass through
me! & the manic imps taking naps on my lips where the price of meant is

                        meat

ENDLESSNESS IS NO DESOLATION

                                     & I am gushing
                 a weird income thus extended within us   gash thru to
rush out an immanence repeating
       lipsynching to the dirty air   I dry heave waves without assistance but
          this too costs something   in the dark thick with lives
lost by the time consumed. Any rip's a threshold of chance of providence through which
others arrive

            to body a bloody roar

                                     & I die die die

The Bright Clear Silence: There must be some sound.

The Distance: Like an intimate sea.

ANY RIP A
THRESHOLD

A RIPTIDE BILE UP & DON'T RUN OFF

COME BACK MARGIN DREST ERRATIC

THESE HEAPS &

HEAPS RETURN

IMPLICIT PLUNGE

RODEO INTO PLUSH

RIDE IAMBIC PIGS

OF RADAR I AM PRONE

OF ROSES INITIATING PEOPLE

OF RANDY IMPERSONAL PIVOTS

OF REOCCURRING INTERLOPING PURITANS

OF RABBITS IMITATING PARLIAMENT

OF MORE IDEALLY SUM INTERSTELLAR
NEW WAVE PARLIAMENT
IMITATING REBEL RABIS IN A
KLEPTOMAGICAL SOCIALISM
OF ECSTATIC INCREASE

OF PURR & WITCH CREASE

OF RAINBOW SPRINKLED LAY & BYE

OF RAPTURE IN PANTS

OF ROT'S IMPLACABLE PLEATS

OF PRIMORDIAL BOOZE CONSUMPTION

IN FANCY RAPTURE PANTS

OF DIFFICULTY IN GITTING

OF GLITTER GLOOM & THE COSMIC TWEENS

OF RUFFLED INTEXTICATED PANTIES

OF ROGUE IDYLLIC PUH-LEEZ

*OF SPLENDOR CUT
BY THUNDER COACH
ITS UNDERFEELING
A BEASTY WONDER GORGE*

*OF RAVINES &
LEAK RANT &
A MUFF IS NEVER A MUFF*

OF RADIO FLOWERS EBBING OUT OF NUMINOUS MOUNDS

OF MOONS & REGIMENTS
& ALEATORY RIMMING

OF RAMROD
HOT TROD
REVVING
IN MACHO
HALO SPEEDO
TRILLING

I GO NILLING SUCKING IN A LOT OF AIR SO AS TO PASS OUT THEN
VEERING OFF A CLIFF

OF SEEPING SONIC SUNS WHILE FALLING

OF FAILING FOR U AGAIN & AGAIN
IN LUV BEYOND ENCROACHING SHIPS

OF OWNERSHIPS

OF DISTANCE SHIPS

OF DELAYSHIPS

OF ALREADY DEADSHIPS

THE WIDENING GAP

THE PLEASANT GASH

*THE HI-LO VERTIGO
RIFF- DIFFICULTY
IN CRAWSING*

*THIS HOST WENT HAPPY HACKED TO PIECES
THIS HOST WENT CRYPTO IN THE MUSEUM OF MELANCHOLY PARTS
THIS HOST WENT ECSTATIC & SAID I LOVE YOU LOCO, LITTLE LOKI
THIS HOST WENT BOWERING IN THE WOODS OF CHANCE
& THIS HOST WENT WA WA WA WA ALL THE WAY CRASH*

THE BIG BOTE SUNCK THO WHO WAWS SAVED

*SUMBODY'S FUTURE WAVES
FROM THE OVERLOOK—*

BRB

RIP

DISTANCE 200 MILES

IMA CLAW SING

IMA KILL UM

IMA RUBY IN THE AMNION

OF RADIOACTIVE IMPOSSIBLE PURIFICATION

OF HINGE & URGE

OF WRITHING IN PUNCAKES

& I'M HUNGRY ALL THE TIME

& MY SELF FOLLERD AFTER

TO BE A HOST INNUMERABLE

I CUT & SEND

I CUT & HIT REPEAT

I CUT & HIT RESENT & COLLAPSE
WHILE SO MANY DISHONOURED LIMBS LASH THE TIDE

I CUT & TRAIPSE & TROLLOP IN LOOPS
THE LOCKS TENDRILLING IN THEIR ORNATE AFTERDEATH

& I WARDROBE
I PETTICOAT & CLAW
I FLIPFLOPS & NAKED IN A WEIRD SCIENCE ARCHIVE
IN WHICH I AM WEEPING

IN WHICH I CAW
IN WHICH I LOL & LOL
& SWILL BILE IN MY VESPERTINE MAW

IN WHICH I SHROUD & CRYPT
I SHROUD & GRIEVE WITH YOU
SO WE MIGHT CORPSE TOGETHER
I SHROUD & UNSHROUD & FLASH
A FORCE BEYOND US
UPTORN & ENTANGLED
AT THE MOUTH OF THE FIRST INDICATION
AURORA OF A NOCTURNAL GAZE

OF GIGANTIC SACS OF CONFOUNDED VOYAGE MILK
ON THE BURSTING VERGE
COMPEL THE PRECIOUS CUT
THE MOST TORTURED CUT OF ALL

OF A BLUE DEEP SO UTTERLY VAST
JOY GOES ELUSIVE
& ITS WISPY WASPY TRACKS OF A RAVENOUS PURSUIT I CUT
& I CUT TO RAVISH RAVENOUS CONFINEMENT
& I RUBBISH

OF LACONIC MAN DOTS IN DESOLATE LOANEDSCAPES

OF SAMURAI PRIESTESS ANA SUROMAI PIGRIDERS

OF IMPROBABLE PEOPLE IN LOST PLACES

OF LIST & STUTTER & ONSLUT

OF PUSSY IN THE LAST PLACE

OF LOST PEOPLE IN IMPROBABLE PLACES

OF DEER WOMEN RUTTING ON ROOF LACE

OF LOSERS & RECONQUISTADORAS & WARPERS & MAMMON

OF PERIPATETIC CATS BEARING MEMOS FROM THE FUTURE

STRAY IN PERPETUITY

INTERSTITIAL INCAMPMENTS

WHERE PAST TENTS MEET PRESENCE

OF A TIME WHEN ALL THE TENSES BLODE DOWN

& SOME HOLDING THARE CATALYTIC PIECES

OF REST IN PIECES IMA LET U FINISH ME WALL OF SOUND

OF ROCKS

OF RENT

OF RIP IT UPPING

OF WANT BLODE DOWN & ALL THAT WAS LEFT

UM

PYRE

DISTANCE 14 MILES

DISTANCE [UNKNOWN QUANTITY OF] GOLDEN BRICKS

OF DIZZY TRICKS

NOT A MOMENT CAUGHT BUT A WILE

COY STUFFING INTO POCKETS

TENDER CUFFING AT THE THROAT

SLIT TO RIP THIS LIST

U WARM & STORMY JUXTOPTICON

OF RADICAL INTERACTIVE PUKING

OF REALLY IMPLOSIVE PULCHRITUDE

OF PUCKS & PARENTS CAMPED ON A SMAWL BRANCH
YOU WOLDENT KNOW IT FROM ANEY OTHER

OF LEVITATING PERIODS

OF UNMET EPOCHS

OF ROCKS IN POCKETS

OF RAVISHING INTENTION PLACE

OF RAID BY INTERVENING PHENOMENA

DISTANCE 20 MILES

OF ROMAN ITALIC PURGENCIES

OF RICH IMPOVERISHMENT PARADE

OF ROWDY INTERPOLATING PIXELS

OF THE SOUND OF DIMINUTIVE SQUARES

OF THE SOUND OF PUBLIC SQUARES OF THE INTERIOR

OF DILATING IN THE SURROUND

SOAKED & STEAMING SAY THRONG THRONG

OF RETCHING IN PACE SAY THRONG

OF THE WORST ROAD SINCE PAWNEESE SAY THRONG

& ALL OF THE RIDERS & ALL OF THE INTANGIBLE & ALL OF THE
PAPERCLITS THRONG

FROM THE FAR REACHES OF LACK

THIS RAW ACHE UNQUOTE

ALMOST EAR

UTTER ERR

RAGGED MARGIN UNDO EROTIC RECEIVER RECEIVE HER

SWOONCLIFF

a body bristles
full of any
one for more
to the point
is noise is
energy & no
one's not in
vited to freak
out or part
icle & smash to
wah full frontal
apoplectic
bloodspurts
in a bout
of base joy
stuck on the
deck till it
's time to
dock to press
their lips in
to the amp
litude of all
-at-once orbits
sounding out the
double signals
of a dead con
sensus—it means
us—rushing into
the lash the
throatslit swine
like a swoonboss
an original
bite like a
jubilant pop
-up book of
phobias full
of songs in
an as of yet in
decipherable m
other tongue

DEAR SEA OUTSIDE,   I'm locked inside an incomplete con
        & therefore free
               to roam

         this being the site where   I smear my face in love's rot
this being the site where distance is an intimacy of its own momentum
            opening in loopholes a spate of
gerunds into some kind a lake becoming
        the clock
is fast but
    its edge, asleep and beyond

    a looming moon pig   full & opal
      mantic pings in the

         disheveled mint

               spring
tender coil summer of violent agitation fall off the edge to build a winter palace in the cliff

(&) *DEAR PIRACY, PARA-SEA,*

I'm on the porch.
I'm in the shadow of community.

I feel totally wrecked and therefore indecipherable. Fontanelle in the shape of campus?
What do we do in this cramped space, these cramps in us, we who get to be in the
correctional workshop the Krampus of voice and form?

Per the typo in the email: how do you benefit form? i.e. how do you benefit tradition?
Insert gif of Judy Garland gilded and swooning flanked by THIS IS HOW MUCH I GIVE
A FUCK. We are in a sea of fuck.

I'm looking for something else. Not me. Fontanelle in the shape of mystery.

How this could only be an artifact of revolt against what I would have once—in an
imagined life—seen as an anachronistic brutality.

Community is the sound the community makes when it means the gold standard.

I guess I want to reclaim the scaffold, the loophole, to reclaim corruption the way your
students suggested we might reclaim killjoy to mean an ample empathy.

Today Maria posted an entry for "loop": *From Middle English loupe ("noose, loop"),
earlier lowp-knot ("loop-knot"), of North Germanic origin, ultimately from Old Norse
hlaup ("a run", literally, "a leap"), used in the sense of a "running knot".*

I'm in the shadow of community
a noose, a loop, a running not—
so what if I'm thick and stupid in my life.

Is that how the line went the one
in the form of no form
feeling big enough? The one
carressing sinful communism
the one eating strawberries
in the cliff palace with the other jewel thieves
in erotic decomposition.
Tender is in circulation
in the shadow of community
you can always live again

MOTHER DEATH

Yeah we come come come
Yeah we come with some some
Get a glass of rum
With a gun and some pun pun
Oh fun fun fun
Let's get 'em undone
M.I.A.

Ironic, but one of the most intimate acts of our body is death.
So beautiful appeared my death—knowing who then I would kiss,
I died a thousand times before I died.
Rabi'ah al-Basri

In language we inhabit a collectivity.

Words come into being via consensus.

More often than not this consensus is long dead.

We speak to each other in a dead consensus
and when we make new words
or transform the use of existent words
we become a part of what will be
a future dead consensus.

When we unhinge words and semantic assemblies
from their normative architecture we are giving
new life to the dead and
by privileging the phonic substance of language
we are making the dead matter.[1]

---

[1] "I have not been interested in the modernist concept of progression, the avant-garde notion of advancing in time. My position has been closer to that of a cosmologist. In other words, we learn by going back in time. The life that we construct is a life that has been out there— we now know—for billions of years." –Jack Whitten, 2013

I want to think about poetry as an uncanny encounter
between the dead and the so-called living and the indecipherable
in a border-space or gutter realm comprised of contamination (cunt animation),
transformation, and failure—a liberating energy.

Both birth and death access this space
it is a threshold, a bardo[2], a cosmic loophole.

Composing a poem means entering this space of polytropic encounter
with what has been written before us. Given the proceedings of history
it happens that these aesthetics and measures of mastery
(not to mention the very notion of mastery) have been determined largely
by an exclusionary, homogenous set of masters and master-makers.

After mechanized time's centuries
of the unheard and the overlooked
—and now in a context of what Kim Gordon has called
MALE WHITE CORPORATE OPPRESSION
—or the FEAR OF A FEMALE PLANET[3]—
who isn't ravenous to read and imagine the alternatives.

[2] "(Perhaps / this is the Bardo // OR // it is another route towards / rebirth or birth
or / simple entertainment / away from intersecting pains the / ones   that only you /
OR / that all others // have felt" –Alice Notley, "PAIN: CONTINUOUS MUTATION"
[3] Kim Gordon, Sonic Youth with Chuck D, "Kool Thing," *Goo.* June 26, 1990 by
Sorcerer Sound Recording Studios and Greene St. Recording, New York.

To do so means inhabiting what Chris Tysh—in her discussion of Alice Notley's Descent of Alette—has called "citational time for this century" of ghosts or

· *Intertextuality*
· *It is first a braid, a weave, a desire to abolish the ring of power.*
· *Gold, emerald, lapis, polished stones, crushed evidence, "cases full of jewels"*
· *"he owns all things," "doesn't he?"*
· *Citational time is non-chronological. A conveyance, a moving track that allows the poet to echo past songs while developing her own measure, "musical intention," her own way to inhabit time, to stress both bridge and what lies below, lost at the bottom of the ditch; something she draws out like a tattered card in the rubble.[4]*

A propulsion through the empire wasteland, a gleaner's wanderlust—always mutant, always in flux—through the kinetic uncanny, a poetry open to haunting, *when home becomes unfamiliar, when your bearings on the world lose direction…. when what's in your blind spot comes into view. Haunting raises specters and it alters the experience of being in time.[5]*

---

[4] Chris Tysh, "Alice Notley: Sheets of Time in Contemporary Lyric Practice," *EOAGH*, 19 May 2012, accessed 8 March 2016, http://eoagh.com/?p=1272.
[5] Avery Gordon, *Ghostly Matters: Haunting and the Sociological Imagination.* (Minneapolis, MN: University of Minnesota Press, 1997) xvi, quoted in k.r.huppert, "Haunting & Utopian States of Being," *Deluge*, Issue One (Fall 2013), 29.

In July 2012 I had recently re-read Bernadette Mayer's *Memory,*
her own July project published in 1975 that sought to document
via photography, sound recordings, & most dominantly, written word[6]
as much of each day as possible.

At the same time Fanny Trollope's *Domestic Manners of the Americans*
kept resurfacing to the top of my bedside pile of books
—maybe compelled by wanderlust & frontiers & the lawlessness they foment,
maybe because I was feeling a stranger in my own country in trying to raise
a new citizen,
maybe, most simply, because I was in love with the name Fanny Trollope
(that it was—to crudely translate—a pussy slut who satirized America).

It wasn't exactly writer's block I was struggling with, but the hungry aporia
of motherhood & poetry, the coincidence of the protective impulse to nurture &
the creative impulse to destroy.

My premise was simple—each day type a single-spaced page
following Bernadette Mayer's premise of writing non-stop whatever dailiness surfaces,
knowing—& here I depart from BM—that I would return to these pages & redact,
distort, or vandalize as necessary.

Whenever I paused, I would pull from Fanny Trollope's chapters on Americans
& integrate her language into my text, using it to spur a continued stream-of-
so-called-consciousness.

It was a way of sharing syntax with her
so that the consciousness was not exclusively my own
nor exclusively hers
but more of a messy permeability
a ncw mcmory of a non-cvcnt
a mutual decomposition.

[6] "& the main thing is we begin with a white sink a whole new language /
is a temptation."

The internal-external r(i)ots.

The in-between language
of revenants collides
with a perverse pleasure
of near-sounds and
puns and estranged,
entangled meaning.

In "Haunting & Utopian State(s) of Being" k.r. huppert writes, *Haunting, as employed
by Avery Gordon, allows us to experience a collapsing of multiple temporalities in on
themselves, where the past, present, and future simultaneously converge and are in
conversation with one another.*

What stains the pages
is something of its own
mutational being.

Far more than a few "voices" at play
there's more of a horde— poems
that bear/bare the traces
or really spaces
of their ghosts.

A spectral palimpsest
about motherhood and death
but
more than being "about"
they are moving about and are driven
by—above all else—
propulsion.

(&) In his essay "On Jean Genet," Edward Said grapples with the ostensible contradictions between the man and the writer and how *[Genet] seemed totally unlike anything of his that [Said] had read, and then discovering in a letter to Roger Blin, [Genet] says in fact that everything he wrote was written 'contre moi-même.'*[7]

Against myself. Anti-self.

There is an uncanny familiarity to this and particularly Said's description of Genet's writing: *you feel that his words, the situations he describes, and the characters he depicts no matter how intensely, no matter how forcefully are provisional. It is always the propulsive force driving him and his characters that Genet's work delivers most accurately.*[8]

Propulsion derives from the Latin *propellere* "drive before (oneself),"[9] and perhaps as a condition of its own force, collapses any spatial organization of past, present, and future, decentering the "I,"

cutting it asunder.

In the margins of Said's essay in *Revolution: A Reader* Lisa Robertson notes, *If we can't live without striving to lose every aspect of our putative self-knowledge in our search for the other, there is no hope for relationship, and hence for politics. It is this crucial loss that the regulatory state would prevent.*[10]

Zurita: *Each one of us is more than an I, each one is a torrent of the deceased that ends in our life just as we end in our descendants. This is what's meant by a tradition and culture: that all those who have preceded us return to speak when we speak, they return to see when we see, feel when we feel. Each one of us is the resurrection of the dead and that miracle is achieved in each second of our lives.*[11]

---

[7] Edward Said, "On Jean Genet" (1990), from *On Late Style*, in *Revolution: A Reader*, compiled and annotated by Lisa Robertson and Matthew Stadler, 593-614, Portland, OR: Publication Studio, 2012.

[8] Said, "Genet," 600.

[9] As if a soccerball, the writing gets touched, propelled, moved this way and that by multiple subjectivities, and a dancer/dance gestalt, the ball seems to acquire a volition of its own. It was a "nice touch" notes Said that a ritual in the remarkable friendship between Genet and Derrida was watching soccer/football matches together.

[10] Lisa Robertson, annotation to "Genet," 603.

[11] Raul Zurita, *Dreams for Kurosawa*, trans. Anna Deeny (Chicago: arrow as aarow, 2012), as quoted in afterword by translator.

(&) How do you write through the Divine Fucked?

Ambivalence?

Polyvalence?

Paradox? Simultaneity?

The frothy contestation of so many dog heads barking, invisible growths on the monumental certainty of the archaic torso?

How can writers overthrow the Tyranny of the I (the cult of personality, I for IMPERIAL) in an empirical reality dedicated to its promise?

Not to be a lone artist inventing in a void,

but something more of a vulnerability oozing through delirious hems.

Inspiration could be called inhaling the memory of an act never experienced. Invention, it must be humbly admitted, does not consist in creating out of voice but out of chaos. Any artist knows these truths, no matter how deeply he or she submerges that knowing.[12]

I'm trying to (w)rite through *that incendiary in-between state, to court anxiety, instability, that glorious fuckedupness.*[13]

---

[12] Jonathan Lethem, "Ecstasy of Influence. A plagiarism," *Harper's*, February 2007, accessed January 20, 2016, http://harpers.org/archive/2007/02/the-ecstasy-of-influence/
[13] Dodie Bellamy, *Academonia* (San Francisco: Krupskaya, 2006), 58.

(&) In a current American context consumer-fetishism and institutional/political abjection
of mothers, caretakers, and children—i.e. the war on women & children—feed a kind
of stereoscopic cultural anxiety.

I joke when I say to sympathetic friends that the most difficult thing about having a kid
is other kids' parents, but the irony of the statement seems to situate it in that culture
of distrust and anxiety by virtue of its own alienating observation,

i.e. I am not immune, simultaneously alien & implicated.

The circuitry of judgment livewires, the lens through which childbirth is seen as a
medical crisis monoliths, and everywhere the micromanagement of space/time of new-
beings microspecializes and in doing so deprives new hearts of the fundamental essence
of human life:

pleasure/pain.

In saying so I find the notion of fearing the loss of one's self in becoming a mother a
product of this ontology.

As if there's a static self to lose. As if death isn't a creative transformation.

There's a poem that refers to the self-consciousness of motherhood as a dark flag
flapping on the edge of things. I don't think I dreamed it, but I also can't locate it.
What poem, what edge? Where?

*Instead of sounding [her]self as to [her] "being," [she] does so concerning her place:
'Where' am I?' instead of 'Who am I?' For the space that engrosses the deject, the excluded
is never one, nor homogeneous, nor totalizable, but essentially divisible, foldable,
and catastrophic.*[14]

---

[14] Julia Kristeva, "An Exile Who Asks, 'Where?,'" *Powers of Horror: An Essay on Abjection*
(New York: Columbia University Press, 1982), 8.

(&) *I do not like them. I do not like their principles. I do not like their manners, I do not like their opinions.* –Fanny Trollope on Americans

Satirical and notorious (in its time), *Domestic Manners of the Americans* chronicles Fanny Trollope's expedition to America with three of her children and a young French artist. They set sail in 1827 with the intention of joining Nashoba, *a utopian community dedicated to educating slaves for their eventual emancipation.*[15] Upon arrival, however, she found a settlement barely populated with *three roofless log cabins in a malaria-ridden swamp.*[16] Completely broke and fearing for the health of her children, she was able to borrow enough money to make it to the then-frontier town of Cincinnati, OH, a.k.a. Porkopolis, the national capitol of pig butchering, in which she confronted the various faces and snouts of the so-called American spirit. As Pamela Neville-Singleton points out in her introduction to the Penguin Classics edition of the book, *Frances Trollope went to the United States, not to gather material for a book, but to seek a temporary shelter from hardship and troubles at home [including significant debt and a husband slowly going mad from mercury poisoning].*[17] The English traveller E.T. Coke, residing state-side when the first American edition appeared, observed:
The commotion it created amongst the good citizens is truly inconceivable....*At every corner of the street, at the door of every petty retailer of information for the people, a large placard met the eye with, 'FOR SALE HERE, WITH PLATES, DOMESTIC MANNERS OF THE AMERICANS, BY MRS. TROLLOPE.'*[18] Not only controversial in America, the book was wildly popular in England.

To 'trollopize,' that is 'to abuse the American nation,' became a recognizable verb in the English language.[19]

[15] Pamela Neville-Sington, introduction to *Domestic Manners of the Americans,* by Fanny Trollope(London: Penguin Books, 1997), xii.
[16] Neville-Sington, introduction, xiii.
[17] Neville-Sington, introduction, viii.
[18] E.T. Coke, quoted in Neville-Sington, introduction, vii.
[19] Neville-Sington, introduction, vii.

(&)   Dear Fanny,

In his seminal 2007 *Vanity Fair* editorial "Why Women Aren't Funny"[20] the late Christopher
Hitchens argues that because of women's biological *unchallengeable authority* in their role
as bearers of life, and their non-need to be funny in courting rites of the species, women can't
play in the halls of jest. And when they do, they are *hefty or dykey or Jewish, or some combo
of the three.* Aside from the suffocatingly normative paradigm—one so outdated it turns to
Kipling and Mencken for support—in which Hitchens asserts, *The chief task in life that a
man has to perform is that of impressing the opposite sex,* he fails to concede that his very defi-
nition of "funny" is self-satisfying and limited to a kind of stale, moldy white (corporate
male) bread, circa 1950.[21]

I'm telling you Hitchens' argument not to shoot an easy target or assault the dead, but to
posit a two-fold argument that
1) his editorial is symptomatic of a greater cultural resistance to satirical gestures in women's
hands, and therefore,
2) the very parameters by which we define cultural authority
        (or the gaze of commentary)
—and humor and irreverence being absolutely essential to its presence—
                are in need of dilation.

                    Love,
                    Cunt

---

[20] Christopher Hitchens, "Why Women Aren't Funny," *Vanity Fair,* January 2007.
[21] Nonetheless, the article seemed to experience a revival upon his death in 2011, at least
    according to my small sample (Facebook feed) in which more than one writer I know
    shared the editorial as a reason to miss Hitchens.

(&) In the improvisational comedy world the pretty versus the funny, a well-worn dichotomy
(as descendent of the virgin vs. the whore binary), often reduces women's identities—i.e. if
you're not pretty, you're funny. These labels can be seen at play in Poetryland (the one so-
called an Industry) but perhaps in even more limiting terms in which the funny is most often
the realm of the testicular and the pretty (or delicate or how Cox characterized Niedecker's
poems with the phrase "tremulous certainty")—an expectation of the female poet.

Perhaps partially in rebellion against my training as a classical ballet dancer, I
actively worked against—and have been interested in writers who complicate and explode—
the feminine pigeonhole (Destroy the pigeonholes! –Tristan Tzara) through a poetics that
embraced the ugly, the incomplete, the awkward, and decay as values of an alternative lyric.

Since that time, inspired my participation in the Flarf Collective, my work has taken on the
funny and the "not-right" as poetic material, but in poems that collide these registers with
other registers of the sincere, the violent, the erotic, and the hysterical.

With this embrace of multiple registers I wanted to collide satirical gestures of mockery,
hyperbole, irreverence, and so forth with the glittering, the sincere, the baroque,
and the tragic.

I'm interested in the threat and inherent risks of such a tonal rumpus.

That these poems in workshops have garnered labels such as "coy," "melodramatic,"
"repetitive," "too much," and "this poem has too many little poems inside it"—by implication
"knocked-up"—seems to underline the risks.

Hitchens himself speculates as to the dangers of women's satire: In his hypothetical vision
of a matriarchal world, he suggests, *It would not have taken women long to work out that
female humor would be the most upsetting of all.*

(&) Why not make upsetting a poetics?
Why not do things backwards or wrong?
Can such energy counteract the catastrophic momentum of a world already topsy-turvy?

Could we call it projectile verse?
Expelling standardized interiority
(the beloved state of the white corporate patriarchy's I)
        in favor of the material realm through
            the kinetic propulsion of word corpses animated
    by the voices of the dead and the living on a stage
        where collision, error, phonetic corrosion, punning, looting,
trollopizing, and play
        are all forces of transformation and revolution—
          a purging of bile—
             via the projectile—

             "The Barf."
And maybe, it might even be fun:
The Barf is feminist, unruly, cheerfully
monstrous. The Barf comes naturally to
women because women like to throw up
fingers down throat, one, two, three, bleh …
The Barf is an upheaval, born of our
hangover from imbibing too much Western
Civ.…the Barf is expansive as the Blob,
swallowing and recontextualizing, spreading
out and engorging. Its logic is associative, it
proceeds by chords rather than single,
discrete notes. Hierarchies jumble in the
thrill, in the imperatives of purge.[22]

---

[22] Dodie Bellamy, *Barf Manifesto*, (New York: Ugly Duckling Presse, 2008).

(&) To a significant extent Flarf
     was all about upsetting and radiated

     a kind of glorious epileptic nihilism.
     In her postscript to *Annoying Diabetic Bitch,*

     the incomparable Sharon Mesmer, who herself
     has been accused of writing "ugly" poetry concludes,

     There's a scene in Werner Herzog's 1979 remake of Nosferatu
     where the citizens of a town gripped by plague dance and sing and carouse

     among corpses rotting and burning in the town square. In a way,
     flarf does pretty much the same thing. But without that awful stench.[23]

     But this was in the early 2000s
     under the insane rule of a Dick

     [Cheney LLC] puppet. Not to say
     our current conditions aren't as problematic,

     they're even MORE SO because of the aura
     of neo-liberalism and its complicity with the rise

     of authoritarianism—now, there's an urgency
     to redefine and re-see reality that was previously obfuscated

     by a totalizing plutocratic charicature. Now more than ever it's time
     to embrace the stench and nurture it and this may mean

     a new kind of tenderness, an other kind of Mother, and it may mean
     eating the dead because they're nutritious.

[23] Sharon Mesmer, *Annoying Diabetic Bitch,* (Cumberland, RI: Combo Books, 2007), 120.

(&) Controversial for their experimental nature and density of references, Ezra Pound's *Cantos* were essentially curated "journal dumps." A canto, the poetic equivalent to chapters in a novel, and such designations as "movement" or "fit,"[24] was used by Pound as a working title. Though his cantos stray from the idea of narrative cohesion, because of "unexpected turns" in his life, the title stuck.[25]

Meanwhile, the sonic sister of "canto"—the cento—is something more of a gathering of the dead, in which the poet is curator or host. I picture Queen Margot and "The Great Ball at Satan's" or Judy Chicago's dinner party.

But what about a cunto? Is it a shadow form? That which is left out, kept apart, in the margins of the tale of the [patriarchy's] tribe? I want to make the cunto not per Pound but punned and complexly femme, a trickster's wandering song, a witch charm confronting the always present past from a compounded and complicated sobjectivity.

In *The Matrixial Borderspace* Bracha Ettinger redefines the female artist: *I call 'woman' this interlaced subjectivity that is not confined to the contours of a one-body with its inside versus outside polarity. This gives rise to an idea of the aritst as working through traces coming through others to whom she is borderlinked. Here in this borderspace, any artist who opens pathways and deepens metamorphoses …thus turns into a woman when she wanders with her spirit's eyes and her erotic antennae in a psychic space and in a world where the gaze is a veil, the touch—the trail of event.*[26] Not this I or that I but the &-between, the encounter.

The ampersand undoing itself
and deforming and reforming and and—
and per se and

"& by itself is and,"
chanted as a mnemonic.
All of the withs in &, the trails

curling in on themselves
and the finite myth of
their convoluted chronologies

holding up and pressing down
twisting, vibrating, sensate,
exchanging.

Time is something more like &.

[24] I hear in these the aura of tantrum, of paroxysm.
[25] *The New Princeton Encyclopedia of Poetry and Poetics*, s.v. "canto."
[25] Bracha L. Ettinger, *The Matrixial Borderspace*, (Minneapolis: University of Minnesota Press, 2006).

120

(&) In "Cybernetics and Ghosts" Italo Calvino offers up a vision of literature as a *combinatorial game that pursues the possibilities implicit in its own material, independent of the personality of the poet, but it is a game that at a certain point is invested with an unexpected meaning, a meaning that is not patent on the linguistic plane on which we were working but has slipped in from another level, activating something that on that second level is of great concern to the author or society.*[27]

A kind of evasive sensitivity with the potential for upset *will be the shock that occurs only if the writing machine is surrounded by the hidden ghosts of the individual and [her] society.*

And is it the shock of wild juxtapositon? Uncanniness? Unidentifiable familiarity? Bad rhyme? The shock of "pollution" historically attributed to death and menses?

Whatever charges of tastelessness or trademark violation may be attached to the artistic appropriation of the media and material environment in which we swim, the alternative—to flinch, or tiptoe away into some ivory tower of irrelevance—is far worse. We're surrounded by signs; our imperative is to ignore none of them.[28]

[27] Italo Calvino, "Cybernetics and Ghosts," *The Uses of Literature* (New York: Harcourt Brace Jovanovich, 1986).

[28] Lethem, "Ecstasy of Influence."

(&) In her Closing Statement on 8 August 2012, Nadezhda Tolokonnikova condemned the "corporate political system" for which the church is proxy and defended Pussy Riot's occupation of the Cathedral of Christ the Savior as a verdict on that system.

In this brilliant and extensive indictment Tolokonnikova invokes, among many other artists, writers, and Jesus,the OBERIU poet Alexander Vvedensky:

Pussy Riot are Vvedensky's students and heirs, she says, His principle of the bad rhyme is dear to us. He wrote, "Occasionally, I think of two different rhymes, a good one and a bad one, and I always choose the bad one because it is always the right one."[29]

I'm not proposing a superlative poetics, but pointing to a necessary one that draws from the ontologies and rites of traditions swept aside in the sterilizing forces of profit-driven, carpe diem history.

The fly-by-night nocturnae, the witches who plaited their hair counterclockwise, who danced in reverse: *What is up, they put down.*[30]

Hans Peter Duerr quotes from seventeeth century texts on witches in Dreamtime: *"at theyr meetings, [they] do all thinges contrary to the custome of Men, dauncing back to back, hip to hip, theyr handes ioyn'd, and making theyr circles backward, to the left hand, with strange phantastique motions of theyr heads, and bodyes."*[31]

& the Heyoka, the sacred clowns of the Lakota, doing everything *backwards-forwards* and *running around with a hammer trying to flatten round and curvy things,* the spirit of thunder and lightning.[32]

& Baubo, who flashed a goddess her pussy as a reminder all things begin and end here.

& the Rabelaises, the Dadaists, the OBERIU, the Baroness, the Flarfists,

and so many more

"The inexplicable is our friend."[33]

---

[29] Maria Alyokhina, Yekaterina Samutsevich, and Nadezhda Tolokonnikova, "Pussy Riot Closing Statements," trans. Bela Sheyavich, N+1 Magazine, accessed February 23, 2016, https://nplusonemag.com/online-only/online-only/pussy-riot-closing-statements/

[30] Petronius, Satyricon, quoted in Hans Peter Duerr, Dreamtime: Concerning the Boundary between Wilderness and Civilization, trans, Felicitas Goodman, (Oxford: Basil Blackwell, 1985), 47.

[31] As quoted in J.P. Cutts, Le rôle de la musique dans les masques de Ben Johnson in Jacquot, J. (ed) Les fêtes de la Renaissance (Paris, 1956) in Duerr, *Dreamtime,* 47.

[32] James R. Walker, Lakota Belief and Ritual, (Lincoln, Nebraska: University of Nebraska Press, 1980)

[33] Tolokonnikova, "Closing Statements" [presumably quoting Vvedensky]

(&)   A poetics that takes chromosomes
      from the Baroness Elsa Von Freytag-Loringhoven's

"Analytical Chemistry of Progeny":

My bawdy spirit is innate—
A legacy from my Dada—
His crude jest bestowed on me
The sparkle of obscenity

My noble mother's legacy
Melancholy—passion—ardour—
Curbed by gentlewoman's reins
Exiled from castle—spoilt gentility

I am—gleaming fruit at the tree top
Fulfilment—brilliant design
Of a thousand-year-old marriage manure
Genius—idiocy—filth—purity.

Whether you love it or turn up your nose
Whether it pleases you or not
It grows—develops—pops off the tree
Circling ball—nude in stockings

What is necessity—Lala! The world—
What Brooklyn Bridge—
Glass-blackened waves and foam.[34]

---

[34] Elsa Von Freytag-Loringhoven, *Body Sweats: The Uncensored Writings of Elsa Von Freytag-Loringhoven*, ed. Irene Gammel & Suzanne Zelazo (Cambridge, Massachusetts: The MIT Press, 2011), 40.

(&) A poetics whose patron saint is Baubo,
the first person to break through Demeter's grief
over the disappearance of her daughter Persephone.
Baubo broke grief by lifting her skirt and flashing the goddess.[35]
And the goddess *laughed.*

Throughout history this moment in the myth has been sanitized
nearly out of existence, and the image of Baubo has mutated
from one of jubilance and earthiness to one of bawdiness and filth.
I'm interested in both manifestations—in the double signals that emerge
in order to survive, something like the Greek word *baubon* which first meant pacifier
but was later used as a term for dildo; or the Greek word *hagos*, which *referred*
to any matter of religious awe or to a sacred being …but was also used as a curse
or an abomination to refer to a polluted person or a defiled place.[36]

In *The Metamorphosis of Baubo* Winifred Lubell writes, *Baubo with her double signals*
was hagos in both meanings of the word. She was sacred—and she was an abomination.
Like the early goddess images she had many aspects. As woman, she contained in her
body the complete round of life, death, and rebirth. Her 'exhibitionism' before Demeter
was a ritual reminder that through their bodies, they each contained the entire mystery
of the creative cycle, i.e. endlessness is no desolation.

Baubo
wet nurse
servant goddess
wife of a pig farmer
pig-rider
crone
bearded lady
witch
night
demon
irresistible
trollop
Isis
Iambe
Bau
trickster
alternatively.

---

[35] In other, presumably later, versions of the story, this gesture is replaced with
and/or mirrored by language, i.e. Baubo makes "wise cracks" (lol) until the goddess
laughs out loud.

[36] Winifred Lubell, *The Metamorphosis of Baubo: Myths of Woman's Sexual Energy*
(Nashville, Tennessee: Vanderbilt University Press, 1994).

(&)   Baubo exposes her vulva
      before Demeter in an act called
      ana-suromai which literally means
      "to lift one's skirt."

      I was recently told by a poetry cop,
      after saying that with this project
      I was thinking about ways to (re-)femme
      the trickster, that the problem
      with the trickster is that
      "it is always against something."
      Exactly.

      But also not true. The trickster
      is often aimless in wandering —
      *Trickster is polytropic, which in its simplest sense means "turning many ways" (though
      the Greek polutropos is also translated "wily," "versatile," and "much-traveled").*[38]
      —wondering, a child of confusion
      and transformation via the unexpected
      and predominantly
      a male archetype.[39]

      Baubo is the lost exception

      *….we have here a female figure of great antiquity, a female flasher as it were, whose
      shamelessness is linked with fertility and the return of the dead, all of which are part of
      the trickster's mythological territory.*[40]

      I want to think about the act of poetry
      as a gloriously awkward gesture
      of ana-suromai in conversation
      with post-partum confusion and grief
      and the anxiety of bringing a girl-child
      into this fucked up patriarchy
      an experience itself warped
      in its own urgency of collapsed time
      and maybe this urgency

---

[37] "[The Wife of Bath] knew much about wandering, by the way."–Chaucer

[38] Lewis Hyde, *Trickster Makes This World: Mischief, Myth, and Art* (New York: North Point Press, 1998), 52.

[39] "Cases such as [Baubo] (or of Sheela-na-gig, another female flasher whose image appeared on churches in Ireland up into the middle ages) suggest that there may have been a tradition of female tricksters that disappeared over the centuries during which Zeus worshippers and Christian 'fathers' were shoring up their dignity." –Hyde, *Trickster Makes This World*, 337.

[40] Hyde, *Trickster Makes the World*, 337.

is a psychic labor in itself
dilating so as to receive
and move toward other possibilities.

This gesture
essential to our psychic survival
is also INCOMPLETE[41]
or contingent upon others
—yes, that there are flashers with us
in solidarity, those before us and those
to come in this nude witch show
but more:

the power of the gesture is in the exchange
what happens *between* Demeter and Baubo
that energy, that
transformation.

[41] "It's not just our *errors* we become brave about, but our projects'—and our own—*incompleteness.* You can stop fearing death, too, if you begin to think of the collective project of being alive in the common world, that one's own end and the end to one's work and one's love is not the end of what is right or good. What needs to go on will." –Anne Boyer, "Tender Theory"

(&)   In "Motherhood Today" Julia Kristeva discusses the ideal of the "good enough mother"[42]
*—she who knows how to leave to make room for pleasure, for the child, for thought.
To leave room, in other words, to disappear.*[43]

Kristeva describes a complex dynamic between the writer Colette and her ideal mother,
her own Sido, who—in one anecdote delayed seeing her own daughter because she was
waiting for a cactus flower to bloom—both disappeared but also through *superb letters*
showed her daughter the infinite pleasures of language:

*Colette ends up saying that the writer of the family is her mother and not Colette
the writer!*

Kristeva asks, *Would not the capacity to share passion through this delight in language
alone be a way of providing a freer more protective maternal presence than does the
overbearing mother whose daughter continues to be dependent on her?*

Kristeva concludes that *by turning all our attention on the biological and social aspects of
motherhood as well as on sexual freedom and equality, we have become the first civiliza-
tion which lacks a discourse on the complexity of motherhood. The imperative,* she sug-
gests, *is to sharpen our understanding of this passion, pregnant with madness and sublim-
ity, because this is what motherhood lacks today.*

[42] "The term…coined by Winnicott, who took this theme further than Freud, nevertheless
runs the risk of playing down the passionate violence of the maternal experience."
-Kristeva, "Motherhood Today"

[43] Julia Kristeva, "Motherhood Today," accessed February 29, 2016,
http://www.kristeva.fr/motherhood.html.

(&)   The tyranny of the I in academia is its singularity, its monolithic finitude & masculinist superego. Notice, writes Lise Haller Baggessen, *how the nurturing nature of the mother is seemingly at odds*[44] *with the singular (masculine) genius on which the mythology of the ivory tower of art and academia is built.*[45]

In a recent report issued by *U.S. News,* "Academia's Baby Penalty," it's suggested that the systemic bias against mothers is not limited to academia alone but a greater cultural phenomenon of *persisting assumptions that so-called career mothers shortchange their babies, their professional competence or both.*[46] These assumptions are by-product of America's *imbecilic capitalist machinery*[47] that is, as a product of its foundational ontology, mysoginistic to the core.

Baggesen picks up Kristeva's thread in the magnificent *Mothernism* and calls for "a new theory of motherhood, a philosophy of motherhood"—in which mother is another sex: *Because if we can accept motherhood as one sex among many, we can perhaps relieve the inevitable burden of motherhood perceived as a stagnant destination. Perhaps we can instead introduce it into a conversation opened up by queer theory, in which categories of gender are more fluid, moving and bleeding into each other.*[48]

A way of thinking that gives form to invisible labor, that does not demonize death, that gives voice to the infinite complexity of relationality, that has so many poetry mothers, that is on its way and always becoming, that is a nascent theory lifting its skirt for poetry and vice versa in perpetuity.

[44] "Men with young children are 35 percent more likely than women with young children to secure tenure-track positions after completing their Ph.D.s. Fathers also outstrip mothers in securing tenure by about 20 percent.//Neither is gender bias alone to blame: Women without children are 33 percent more likely than women with children to secure tenure-track faculty positions."—Sandra Waxman & Simone Ipsa-Landa, "Academia's Baby Penalty," *U.S. News & World Report,* February 11, 2016, accessed February 29, 2016, http://www.usnews.com/opinion/knowledge-bank/articles/2016-02-11/academia-must-correct-systemic-discrimination-and-bias-against-mothers.

[45] Lise Haller Baggesen, *Mothernism* (Chicago: Green Lantern Press, 2014), 84.

[46] "For example, Princeton University students were asked recently to consider several fictitious consultants including two new parents who continued to work. The only difference between these new parents was their gender – yet the students described 'Kate' as considerably less competent than 'Dan.'"—Waxman & Simone, "Academia's Baby Penalty"

[47] Thx, Cixous.

[48] Baggesen, *Mothernism,* 84, 82.

may it be undone/unfinished
compounded & complicated
by the dead/living
through play/defiance—

a something else to say
a cunnilingua
of mutational, material magic

Sources

Baggesen, Lise Haller. *Mothernism.* Chicago: Green Lantern Press, 2014.

Bellamy, Dodie. *Academonia.* San Francisco: Krupskaya, 2006.

Bellamy, Dodie. *Barf Manifesto.* New York: Ugly Duckling Presse, 2008.

Calvino, Italo. "Cybernetics and Ghosts." *The Uses of Literature.* New York: Harcourt Brace Jovanovich, 1986.

Duerr, Hans Peter. *Dreamtime: Concerning the Boundary Between Wilderness and Civilization.* Translated by Felicitas Goodman. Oxford: Basil Blackwell, 1985.

Ettinger, Bracha. *The Matrixial Borderspace.* Minneapolis: University of Minnesota Press, 2006.

Von Freytag-Loringhoven, Elsa. *Body Sweats: The Uncensored Writings of Elsa Von Freytag-Loringhoven.* Edited by Irene Gammel & Suzanne Zelazo. Cambridge, Massachusetts: The MIT Press, 2011.

Gordon, Avery. *Ghostly Matters: Haunting and the Sociological Imagination.* Minneapolis: University of Minnesota Press, 1997.

Gordon, Kim. *Goo.* Sonic Youth with Chuck D. Sorcerer Sound Recording Studios and Greene St. Recording. 9 24297-D2, 1990.

Hitchens, Christopher. "Why Women Aren't Funny." *Vanity Fair* January 2007.

Hyde, Lewis. *Trickster Makes This World: Mischief, Myth, and Art.* New York: North Point Press, 1998.

huppert, k.r. "Haunting & Utopian States of Being." *Deluge* 1 (2013): 29.

Kristeva, Julia. "Motherhood Today." Accessed February 29, 2016. http://www.kristeva.fr/motherhood.html.

Kristeva, Julia. *Powers of Horror: An Essay on Abjection.* New York: Columbia University Press, 1982.

Lethem, Jonathan. "Ecstacy of Influence. A plagiarism." *Harper's.* February 2007. Accessed January 20, 2016. http://harpers.org/archive/2007/02/the-ecstacy-of-influence/.

Lubell, Winifred. *The Metamorphosis of Baubo: Myths of Woman's Sexual Energy.* Nashville, Tennessee: Vanderbilt University Press, 1994.

Mayer, Bernadette. *Memory.* Plainfield, Vermont: North Atlantic Books, 1975.

Mesmer, Sharon. *Annoying Diabetic Bitch.* Cumberland, Rhode Island: Combo Books, 2007.

Notley, Alice. "PAIN: CONTINUOUS MUTATION," *We Are So Happy to Know Something,* edited by Stephanie Anderson & MC Hyland. Volume 2 (2011): 5.

Robertson, Lisa & Matthew Stadler, eds. *Revolution: A Reader.* Portland, Oregon: Publication Studio, 2012.

Said, Edward. "On Jean Genet." In *Revolution: A Reader,* compiled and annotated by Lisa Robertson and Matthew Stadler, 593 – 614. Portland, Oregon: Publication Studio 2012. Originally published in Edward Said, *On Late Style: Music and Literature Against the Grain* (New York: Pantheon Books, 2006).

Tolokonnikova, Nadezhda, Maria Alyokhina, and Yekaterina Samutsevich. "Pussy Riot 23 Statements." Translated by Bela Sheyavich. *N+1 Magazine.* Accessed February 23, 2016. https://nplusonemag.com/online-only/pussy-riot-closing-statements.

Trollope, Fanny. *Domestic Manners of the Americans.* Ed. Pamela Neville-Sington. London: Penguin Books, 1997.

Tysh, Chris. "Alice Notley: Sheets of Time in Contemporary Lyric Practice." *EOAGH,* 19 May 2012. Accessed 8 March 2016. http://eoagh.com/?p=1272.

Walker, James R. *Lakota Belief and Ritual.* Lincoln, Nebraska: University of Nebraska Press, 1980.

Waxman, Sandra & Simone Ipsa-Landa. "Academia's Baby Penalty." *U.S. News & World Report,* February 11, 2016. Accessed February 29, 2016. http://www.usnews.com/opinion/knowledge-bank/articles/2016-02-11/academia-must-correct-systemic-discrimination-and-bias-against-mothers.

Whitten, Jack. "Jack Whitten: 50 Years of Painting." Walker Art Center. Minneapolis. September 13, 2015 – January 24, 2016.

Zurita, Raúl. *Dreams for Kurosawa.* Translated by Anna Deeney. Chicago: arrow as aarow, 2012.

**Images

4 American Colony. Photo Dept., photographer. *The terrible plague of locusts in Palestine, March-June 1915. Cloud of locusts coming over the horizon.* 1915. Image. Retrieved from the Library of Congress, https://www.loc.gov/item/mpc2004004217/PP/. (Accessed September 5, 2016.)

7 American Colony. Photo Dept., photographer. *The terrible plague of locusts in Palestine, March-June 1915. Cloud of locusts coming over the horizon.* 1915. Image. Retrieved from the Library of Congress, https://www.loc.gov/item/mpc2004004217/PP/. (Accessed September 5, 2016.)

11 American Colony. Photo Dept., photographer. *Dead Sea album prepared for the Palestine Potash Ltd. Night falls over the camp.* [Between 1934 and 1937] Image. Retrieved from the Library of Congress, https://www.loc.gov/item/mpc2004002811/PP/. (Accessed September 7, 2016.)

15 Hine, Lewis Wickes, photographer. *A little spinner in the Mollahan Mills, Newberry, S.C. She was tending her "sides" like a veteran, but after I took the photo, the overseer came up and said in an apologetic tone that was pathetic, "She just happened in." Then a moment later he repeated the information. The mills appear to be full of youngsters that "just happened in," or "are helping sister."* Dec. 3, 08. Witness Sara R. Hine. Location: Newberry, South Carolina / Photo by Lewis W. Hine. December 3, 1908. Image. Retrieved from the Library of Congress, https://www.loc.gov/item/ncl2004001280/PP/. (Accessed September 4, 2016.)

22 Historic American Engineering Record, Creator. *Over-the-Horizon Backscatter Radar Network, Christmas Valley Radar Site Transmit Sector Six Transmitter Building, On unnamed road west of Lost Forest Road, Christmas Valley, Lake County, OR.* Documentation Compiled After, 1968. PDF. Retrieved from the Library of Congress, https://www.loc.gov/item/or0564/. (Accessed September 5, 2016.)

26 Van Vechten, Carl, photographer. *[The witch's house, Maine].* 1936. Image. Retrieved from the Library of Congress, https://www.loc.gov/item/2004663860/. (Accessed September 7, 2016.)

30 *Tornado, Lebanon, Kansas.* ca. 1902. Image. Retrieved from the Library of Congress, https://www.loc.gov/item/96512152/. (Accessed September 4, 2016.)

43 Bradford, William, Pierce, William H, photographer. *[Iceberg in the Atlantic Ocean, off the coast of Labrador].* [1864] Image. Retrieved from the Library of Congress, https://www.loc.gov/item/2012645577/. (Accessed September 5, 2016.)

46 *Seagulls hovering hopefully as the Norwegian fishermen in Scotland gut fish ready for the market.* Between 1941 and 1943?. Image. Retrieved from the Library of Congress, https://www.loc.gov/item/owi2001046367/PP/. (Accessed September 5, 2016.)

54 American Colony. Photo Dept, photographer. *Flight to Ma'an el-Hadj, Petra, Wadi Rum and Akaba. Nageb area. Weird scene of desolation S.E. of Nageb Ma'an.* [?, 1932] Image. Retrieved from the Library of Congress, https://www.loc.gov/item/mpc2010007830/PP/. (Accessed September 5, 2016.)

60 American Colony. Photo Dept., photographer. *Wild flowers of Palestine. Field of yellow carrot Daucus aureus Desf.* [approximately to 1920, 1900] Image. Retrieved from the Library of Congress, https://www.loc.gov/item/mpc2004004760/PP/. (Accessed September 6, 2016.)

65 Carpenter, Frank G. , Collector. *[Chile - Aconcagua Valley].* [Between 1890 and 1930] Image. Retrieved from the Library of Congress, https://www.loc.gov/item/2001704585/. (Accessed September 4, 2016.)

70 American Colony. Photo Dept., photographer. *[Air views of Palestine. Various points of interest around Jerusalem. Tell el-Nasbeh. Indentified i.e., Identified as Mizpah].* [1931] Image. Retrieved from the Library of Congress, https://www.loc.gov/item/mpc2010007770/PP/. (Accessed September 5, 2016.)

75 American Colony. Photo Dept., photographer. *Wild flowers of Palestine. Field of yellow carrot Daucus aureus Desf.* [approximately to 1920, 1900] Image. Retrieved from the Library of Congress, https://www.loc.gov/item/mpc2004004760/PP/. (Accessed September 6, 2016.)

99 Detroit Publishing Co., Publisher. *Surf.* [Between 1900 and 1905] Image. Retrieved from the Library of Congress, https://www.loc.gov/item/det1994018997/PP/. (Accessed September 5, 2016.)

104 *[Woman and Girl on Rock by Ocean].* [-10, ca. 1900] Image. Retrieved from the Library of Congress, https://www.loc.gov/item/2002699164/. (Accessed September 5, 2016.)

129 *Along the Maine coast.* ca. 1900. Image. Retrieved from the Library of Congress, https://www.loc.gov/item/92514883/. (Accessed September 11, 2016.)

144 Lomen Bros, photographer. *Positions of sun at hours 10 and 11 a.m., 12 m., and 1 and 2 p.m. on Dec. 28th, 1910 from Nome, Alaska.* ca. 1911. Image. Retrieved from the Library of Congress, https://www.loc.gov/item/99614597/. (Accessed September 6, 2016.)

Acknowledgments

Versions of some of these poems have appeared on the Bloof blog, in *Delirious Hem's* Advent feature, *Gesture Magazine, Ocean State Review, Tarpaulin Sky,* and the chapbook *Poetry for Your Momma* (issued by the Cornell College Center for the Literary Arts). An earlier version of the messay "Mother Death" was featured at Montevidayo (RIP). *ANY RIP A THRESHOLD* was issued as a chapbook by Shirt Pocket Press. Thank you, University of Minnesota, for a Marcella DeBourg Fellowship to "give creative expression to women's lives."

This book would not exist without my kin Erik Brandt, B, & C, in the nest of love and difficult/vital mutation; the tendrils/tender entanglements of my weird sisters, Carrie Lorig, Bridget Mendel Lee, Sarah Fox, Feng Sun Chen; my poetry mother Maria Damon and co-unicorn Jenny Schmid at the Department of Bohemian Studies; the silver planet ~~book club~~ life raft Emily Fedoruk and Erin Trapp; my poetry brother Michael Sikkema; Susana Gardner like the beautiful daughter of Befana; and all of the teachers/students of the shadow school, marooned as we are. I am endlessly grateful.

Colophon

ENDLESSNESS IS NO DESOLATION
© 2016 Elisabeth Workman

Graphic Design: Erik Brandt/Typografika
Minneapolis, MN Estados Unidos
http://typografika.com

Cover image: Lomen Bros, photographer. *Positions of sun at hours 10 and 11 a.m., 12 m., and 1 and 2 p.m. on Dec. 28th, 1910 from Nome, Alaska.* ca. 1911. Image. Retrieved from the Library of Congress, https://www.loc.gov/item/99614597/. (Accessed September 6, 2016.)

This book is set largely in Life (Linotype), by Francesco Simoncini. Berthold Akzidenz Grotesk (Berthold), by Hermann Berthold, is also used.

Published by Dusie Press
Kingston, Rhode Island USA
http://dusie.org

ISBN: 978-1-944253-03-5
1. American poetry–21st century.
2. Poets, American–21st century.